TRAVE
THEAT

Traverse Theatre Company

The Tree of Knowledge

By Jo Clifford

Cast

David Hume	Gerry Mulgrew
Adam Smith	Neil McKinven
Eve	Joanna Tope

Director	Ben Harrison
Assistant Director	Ali Maclaurin
Video Designer	Tim Reid
Composer	David Paul Jones
Lighting Designer	Jeanine Davis

Company Stage Manager	Gemma Smith
Deputy Stage Manager	Elaine Diffenthal
Assistant Stage Manager	Lee Davis
Wardrobe Supervisor	Rebecca Fenner Evans

First performed at the Traverse Theatre
8 December 2011

A Traverse Theatre Company Commission

THE TRAVERSE

The Traverse has an unrivalled reputation for producing contemporary theatre of the highest quality, invention and energy, and for its dedication to new writing.
(Scotland on Sunday)

The Traverse is Scotland's new writing Theatre. From its conception in 1963, it has embraced a spirit of innovation and risk-taking that launched the careers of many of Scotland's best-known writers including John Byrne, David Greig, David Harrower and Liz Lochhead. The Traverse fulfils the crucial role of providing the professional support and expertise to ensure the development of a dynamic theatre culture for Scotland. It commissions and develops new plays or adaptations from contemporary playwrights. It produces, on average, six Traverse Theatre Company productions or co-productions per year. It also presents a large number of productions from visiting companies from across the UK and beyond. These include new plays, adaptations, dance, physical theatre, puppetry and contemporary music.

The Traverse is a pivotal venue in Edinburgh and this is particularly the case during the Edinburgh Festival in August.

The Traverse is also the home of the Manipulate Visual Theatre Festival, the Bank of Scotland Imaginate Festival and the Traverse's own autumn Festival.

A Rolls-Royce machine for promoting new Scottish drama across Europe and beyond. (The Scotsman)

The Traverse's work with young people is of major importance and takes the form of encouraging playwriting through its flagship education project, Class Act, as well as the Young Writers' Group. Class Act recently celebrated its twenty-first anniversary and has given school pupils the opportunity to develop their plays with professional playwrights and work with directors and actors to see the finished pieces performed on stage at the Traverse. The hugely successful Young Writers' Group is open to new writers aged 18–25. Scribble offers an after-school playwriting and theatre-skills workshop for 14–17 year olds. Both programmes are led by professional playwrights.

Traverse Theatre (Scotland) Limited, registered in Scotland SC 076037.
Registered Charity No. SC 002368, VAT reg. no. 356 0682 47.
Registered Office: Traverse Theatre, Cambridge Street, Edinburgh, EH1 2ED.

COMPANY BIOGRAPHIES

Jo Clifford (Writer)
Jo Clifford is an award-winning playwright, translator, poet and performer, who has also worked as a journalist and academic. She has written and adapted around eighty works for theatre, opera, film and television. Jo was instrumental in establishing the reputation of the Traverse Theatre Company in the 1980s, with the plays *Losing Venice*, *Light in the Village*, *Inés de Castro*, *Playing with Fire* and *Lucy's Play*. Jo's most recent work for the Traverse was in 1993 with *Anna* (co-produced with Edinburgh International Festival). *The Tree of Knowledge* was commissioned by the Traverse and created while Jo was Creative Fellow at the Institute of Advanced Studies in the Humanities at the University of Edinburgh. Other theatre work includes: *Life is a Dream* (Edinburgh International Festival); *Anna Karenina*, *Faust* and *Every One* (Royal Lyceum Theatre, Edinburgh); *The Gospel According to Jesus, Queen of Heaven* (Tron Theatre); *The Cherry Orchard*, *The Seagull* (Theatre Alba); *Queen Echinacea* (Boilerhouse Theatre Company); *Life is a Dream* (Rough Magic); *Great Expectations* (Northern Stage); *Celestina* (Edinburgh International Festival/Birmingham Rep); *Sitios*, *S.D.O*, *Bintou*, *Bazaar* (Royal Court); *Tchaikovsky and the Queen of Spades*, *Charles Dickens: The Haunted Man*, *Wuthering Heights*, *La Vie de Bohème* (Pitlochry Festival Theatre) and *Great Expectations* (TAG). Radio plays include: *La Princesse de Cleves*, *Spam Fritters*, *The Chimes*, *Madeleine*, *Baltasar and Blimunda*, *The Constant Prince*, *Torquemada*, *Inés de Castro*, *Letters from a Strange Land*, *The Leopard*, *Writing Home to Mother*, *La Vie de Bohème*. As a performer, her work includes: *Leave To Remain* (a theatre ritual for the bereaved, which she devised and performs with Suzanne Dance); *The Gospel According to Jesus, Queen Of Heaven* (which she has just performed as part of the Homotopia Festival, Liverpool) and *Sex, Chips and the Holy Ghost* (which she devised with David Walshe and Susan Worsfold and will be performing with them at Òran Mór in February 2012). She is the proud father of two amazing grown-up daughters.

Jeanine Davis (Lighting Designer)
Jeanine's lighting design work for the Traverse: *Nova Scotia*. Other theatre work includes: *Lifeboat*, *Hansel and Gretel* (Catherine Wheels); *The Curse of the Starving Class*, *The Man Who Had All the Luck* (Royal Lyceum, Edinburgh); *The Testament of Cresseid* (Edinburgh International Festival); *The Ducky* (Borderline); *A Christmas Carol* (Chichester Festival Theatre); *Privates on Parade* (West Yorkshire Playhouse); *A Streetcar Named Desire* (Perth Theatre); *The Unconquered* (Byre Theatre/'Brits off Broadway, New York). She has worked extensively in dance including: *Proband* (Caroline Bowditch); *Found, Almost But Not Quite* (Curious Seed/Dance Base); *Raw* (Fidget Feet); *Off Kilter* (Dance Base); *Uncanny* (X Factor Dance Company). Jeanine is also a Pilates teacher.

Ben Harrison (Director)

Ben is the Co-Artistic Director of Grid Iron, and from 2004–2008 was also a director of the Dutch theatre company MUZtheater. Ben's work for the Traverse: *Spring Awakening* (co-produced with Grid Iron). For Grid Iron: *What Remains, Decky Does a Bronco, Huxley's Lab* (co-produced with Lung Ha's Theatre Company), *Barflies, Tryst, Yarn* (co-produced with Dundee Rep), *Once Upon A Dragon* (co-produced with Imaginate), *Roam* (co-produced with National Theatre of Scotland and BAA Edinburgh International Airport), *The Devil's Larder, Those Eyes, That Mouth, Variety, Fermentation, Monumental, Gargantua, The Bloody Chamber* and *Clearance.* Other work includes: *This Twisted Tale* (Paper Doll Militia); *You Tell Us What Was We Tell You What Is* (National Theatre of Scotland Learn); *The Tailor of Inverness* (Dogstar) and *Peter Pan* (360 Entertainment). Ben is currently developing a new piece from Lebanon, *Bint Jbeil.* From 2000–2002 he was Associate Director (Education) of the Almeida Theatre in London, where he directed *Caledonian Road, A Chaste Maid in Cheapside, The Whizzkid, Decky Does A Bronco* (co-produced with Grid Iron), *Ghost Ward, The Last Valentine* and *Into Our Dreams.* Future projects include: *Bedsheets (Sharashif)* in collaboration with Shams Theatre, Beirut. www.benharrison.org

David Paul Jones (Composer & Sound Designer)

David Paul Jones studied classical piano and composition at the RSAMD in the early 1990s. Theatre soundtracks for National Theatre of Scotland include: *The Missing, Elizabeth Gordon Quinn, Mary Queen of Scots Got Her Head Chopped Off, Our Teacher's A Troll, Something Wicked This Way Comes* (co-produced with Catherine Wheels) and *Dolls* (co-produced with Hush Productions). He has been a member of the Grid Iron creative team since 2003 composing and performing soundtracks for productions including: *Those Eyes, That Mouth, The Devil's Larder, Barflies* and *What Remains.* Soundtracks for children and young people's theatre include: *The Attic* (Imaginate); *The Songbird* (Giant Productions); *Pobby & Dingan* and *Caged* (Catherine Wheels). His album *Something There* is released on Linn Records. His work has received several nominations at the CATS Awards and he is a finalist in the Glenfiddich Spirit of Scotland Awards for Music.

Ali Maclaurin (Design)

Ali trained in theatre design in Edinburgh and Croydon. She has designed, devised, made, facilitated and taught all over the country. In the 1990s she was resident designer with the Belgrade Theatre, Coventry and in 2004 she set up a costume design degree at Queen Margaret University. Design work for the Traverse: *Spring Awakening* (co-produced with Grid Iron). Other design work includes: *BabyO* (Scottish Opera); *What Remains* (Grid Iron); *The Tailor of Inverness* (Dogstar); *Quangle Wangle* (Derby Live); *Acoustic/Electric* (Skinreach); *The Singing Nun* (Nina and Frederick Productions). Ali has worked on projects for Scottish Opera, TAG, Battersea Arts Centre and designed several shows for Licketyspit as well as teaching stage design part time at Adam Smith College.

Neil McKinven (*Adam Smith*)
Neil's work for the Traverse: *The Last Witch* (co-produced with Edinburgh International Festival), *Wiping My Mother's Arse*, *Widows* and *Abandonment*. Other theatre work includes: *A Doll's House* (Dundee Rep); *Caledonia* and *Rapture* (National Theatre of Scotland); *Curse of the Starving Classes* (Royal Lyceum, Edinburgh); *Of Mice and Men* (Perth Theatre) and *The Comedy of Errors*, *Twelfth Night* (Royal Shakespeare Company). Television and film work includes: *The Body Farm*, *Case Histories*, *Single Father*, *Scottish Killers*, *Rebus*, *Taggart*, *Hallam Foe* and *A is for Acid*.

Gerry Mulgrew (*David Hume*)
Gerry is an actor, writer, director and musician. He was born in Glasgow and educated at Glasgow University where he graduated with an MA in French and Philosophy. Acting work for the Traverse: *Nova Scotia*. Other acting work includes: *The Memorandum*, *The Government Inspector*, (Communicado); *Federer V Murray* (Òran Mór). For Dundee Rep: *The Visit*, *Ubu The King*, *Peer Gynt* (co-produced with National Theatre of Scotland – CATS Award for Best Actor). Gerry co-founded Communicado in 1983, and has since directed forty original plays for the company including: *Calum's Road*, *Tall Tales* (co-produced with National Theatre of Scotland), *The Government Inspector*, *Jock Tamson's Bairns*, *The House With the Green Shutters*, *Cyrano de Bergerac*, *The Cone Gatherers*, *The Suicide*, *Mary Queen of Scots Got Her Head Chopped Off* and *A Wee Home from Home*. Most recently he has directed *Calum's Road* and *Tall Tales* for Communicado/NTS.

Tim Reid (Video Design)
Tim has designed video effects and playback systems for shows that range from experimental small-scale works to full-scale opera, ballet and theatre productions. He has designed video for Vox Motus, DV8 Physical Theatre, National Theatre of Scotland, The Royal Ballet, The Edinburgh International Festival, David Leddy, Dogstar, Theatre By The Lake, Random Accomplice, Dancebase and TAG. He has worked as Head of Video for the National Theatre of Scotland and toured internationally with DV8 Physical Theatre.

Joanna Tope (*Eve*)
Joanna Tope studied Drama at Manchester University. *The Tree of Knowledge* will be Joanna's first time working with Traverse Theatre Company. Recent theatre work includes: *The Promise/Promises Promises* (Random Accomplice; Outstanding Solo Performance Drama Desk Nomination 2011); *Death of a Salesman*, *A Christmas Carol*, *Dangerous Liaisons* (Royal Lyceum, Edinburgh); *Oedipus*, *A Taste of Honey*, *Cheri*, *Peer Gynt* (Citizens Theatre); *Frozen* (Rapture); *Wit* (Stellar Quines). Television work includes: *Monarch of the Glen*, *The Key*, *Emmerdale Farm*. She has recorded many plays and short stories for BBC Radio, including several Jo Clifford plays, and books for Audio Go.

SUPPORT THE TRAVERSE

We would like to thank the following
corporate sponsors for their recent support

For their generous support, the Traverse thanks our Devotees 2006–2011

Joan Aitken, Stewart Binnie, Katie Bradford, Fiona Bradley,
Adrienne Sinclair Chalmers, Lawrence Clark, Adam Fowler, Joscelyn Fox,
Caroline Gardner, John Knight OBE, Iain Millar, Gillian Moulton, Helen
Pitkethly, Michael Ridings, Bridget Stevens

TRAVERSE THEATRE CLUB
Celebrating the Traverse Theatre 1963–2013

The Traverse extends a very warm welcome and thanks to its new
Traverse Theatre Club members for their support:

Lawnmarket: Joan Aitken, Stewart Binnie, Katie Bradford, Lawrence
Clark, Joscelyn Fox, Iain Millar, Gillian Moulton,
Helen Pitkethly, Bridget Stevens.
Grassmarket: John Knight OBE, Ged Welch,
Dr Kenneth Wilkie.
Saltire Traverse 1: Jane Attias, Elaine Cameron,
Kristine Sander, Georgia Thornton, Dr Peng Lee Yap.

Help us to continue to shape the future cultural landscape of Scotland with
new work that resonates across the world and join the Traverse Theatre
Club. You'll be in good company!

For further information about membership levels please email:
theatreclub@traverse.co.uk or call Jennifer Deane, Box Office and
Club Manager on 0131 228 1404

Emerging Playwright on Attachment post supported by Playwrights'
Studio, Scotland as a Partnership Project

Pearson Playwright supported by **Pearson**

**For their continued generous support of Traverse
productions, the Traverse thanks**
Camerabase, Paterson SA Hairdressing, Stems Florist

**The Traverse Theatre's work
would not be possible without the support of**

**For their help on *The Tree of Knowledge*, the company would
like to thank**
Royal Lyceum Theatre, Tron Theatre, Citizens Theatre,
Pitlochry Festival Theatre, Dundee Rep

TRAVERSE THEATRE – THE COMPANY

THE TREE OF KNOWLEDGE

Jo Clifford

Introduction

I've never written a play about a philosopher before.

Didn't know how to do it. But then I always knew I'd think of something. That's one good thing about having written about eighty plays: you have a sense you can tackle anything.

The nice thing about this commission was that it came with a fellowship. It's jolly good, being a creative fellow. Especially at IASH – The Institute for Advanced Studies in the Humanities – at Edinburgh University.

I had a lovely room overlooking The Meadows. I had free photocopying. And envelopes. And fantastic company. Sociologists and culture historians and feminist thinkers and philosophers too. Amazing eye-opening lectures and seminars. Access to a real intellectual community which, now that universities are being reduced to anti-educational degree factories, feels somehow miraculous.

I started to read about Hume. The first day, I hit this difficulty: I didn't really understand what he was saying. When I read his biography, I could relate to him as a human being, but the trouble with that was that I didn't want to write anything biographical. I didn't want periwigs and crinolines.

I escaped into writing another play altogether. A play called *The Tree of Life*, which I'd first written some years ago for the Brunton Theatre in Musselburgh. The Scottish Arts Council had given me funds to write the play but taken away funds from the theatre so they couldn't produce it.

I wrote it anyway: a ninety-minute piece with a cast of six (three men, three women) which needed more work. I thought I'd rewrite it, expand it for a bigger theatre, and then it would make a companion for this play. Which would be *The Tree of Knowledge*.

And how nice to have a title.

I enjoyed rewriting *The Tree of Life* – it tells the story of the apprentice pillar in Rosslyn Chapel, and all the characters come out of the audience (and go back into it at the end), and the master mason falls in love with the apprentice and the women tear a male character to pieces.

It was all very passionate and a bit mad, too; and I imagined *The Tree of Knowledge* would work with the same cast, and they could be played in repertoire, somehow, one day, maybe, and because the Knowledge Tree was all about philosophy it would be quite a cool and rational affair.

Then someone very special happened to tell me about how she'd worked in a computer factory in Glenrothes, in Fife, in the days when it was known as Silicon Glen, and I suddenly saw all kinds of connection with Glenrothes new town and Edinburgh new town; and the revolution in thinking implied by the development of computers connected to the revolution in thinking brought about by Hume's philosophy (which I still didn't really understand), and the economic theories of his friend Adam Smith.

So now I had three characters, Hume, Smith, and the woman in the computer factory, whose name was obviously Eve, and I had the first scene too. Set on an assembly line, obviously, because Smith, in a famous passage, described very beautifully how assembly-line working can transform workers' productivity.

The only problem was that I couldn't for the life of me understand what David Hume and Adam Smith were doing working in a computer factory in Glenrothes in 1976.

Or who the other three characters were. And I still couldn't understand Hume's philosophy.

The other three characters wouldn't say a word. They just stood around in my imagination, voiceless and glum. So they went. And then it somehow became clear that Smith wasn't there, either.

So where was Smith? I had to write the previous scene to find out. And the scene before that...

Meantime I'd given up trying to understand Hume's philosophy. I was reading his essays instead. And they are a delight: elegant, witty, provocative and wise.

In one of them he proves with the greatest beauty and elegance that life after death is an absolute impossibility.

So imagine how cross he would be if he woke up after dying and discovered he'd been wrong.

So I did. And that was really the first scene.

I can never plan plays. Obviously. All I can do is become the characters and see what they have to say for themselves and what they want to do. And become the actors playing them on stage, too, and saying lines I would like to say myself in scenes I would like to be in.

But I'm also being the audience, and that's maybe the most important bit, because that's how I get to write it all down. And also try to do my best to make sure that what's happening is a play that I would find it a pleasure to watch.

Which is not quite the same as understanding what's going on. I couldn't really make head or tail of this play until about two days before I was due to hand it in. Which is a bit ironic, really, since two of its main characters are famous for being such fantastic thinkers and such rational and enlightened human beings.

I'm not sure why I suddenly remembered *The Tibetan Book of the Dead*, but I did. I read it years ago, and Timothy Leary's version of it, too, just before I took LSD. And me and Suzanne Dance had tried to use it for our theatre ritual to help the bereaved, *Leave To Remain*, and then abandoned it because we couldn't really understand it.

But suddenly these ancient Tibetan instructions, designed to be read over a corpse immediately after death because they give the dead person vital instructions as to how to comport themselves in the next life, they suddenly made perfect sense.

My new play, I understood with utter clarity, is set in the *Bardo*. In the intermediate space between death and the next life: when what we experience is a reflection of the state of consciousness we developed when we were still alive.

Not that anyone necessarily needs to know that: but it comforted me to know that I did.

As I write this, I'm about to go into rehearsals. With the script in the form you now read it.

I think it will work, more or less. But have no real way of knowing: and won't know, until the rehearsals are over. By which time it may look very different.

But whatever form it reaches you, I hope it gives much pleasure.

Jo Clifford
Edinburgh, 6 November 2011

Author's Note

This play was commissioned by the Traverse Theatre, Edinburgh.

While researching it I was Creative Fellow at the Institute for Advanced Studies in the Humanities at the University of Edinburgh. It was an intellectually stimulating and creatively profound experience; and I am grateful to its fellows and staff.

I am particularly grateful to Dr Peter Millican of Hertford College, Oxford. His website davidhume.org is a fantastic resource for all things to do with David Hume.

I am also grateful to Professor Deirdre McCloskey of the University of Illinois, Chicago, for her insights into Adam Smith.

To Marie.

Who ate the apple too.

Characters

EVE, *in middle age*
DAVID HUME, *a bit older*
ADAM SMITH, *a bit younger*

Note on the Text

All I ask of this performance space is that it be interesting.

And preferably unusual.

That it is not ashamed to be a theatre.

I have a feeling a screen may be useful.

One that can receive projections.

I also think the cast are already on stage.

Each cast member has a chair: Hume's is elegant. Smith's is plain.

Eve's is round and hangs suspended.

The actors greet each other and check their props.

They're a bit like members of an orchestra before the concert starts.

When everything's ready, they wish each other good fortune...

...And launch into the prologue.

This text went to press before the end of rehearsals and so may differ slightly from the play as performed.

PROLOGUE

At first the houselights stay on.

The ACTORS *greet the audience.*

HUME   David Hume, philosopher. At your service.

SMITH   Adam Smith, economist. Not at your service.
The market is not at your service.
You are at the service of the market.

EVE   Two famous people and someone ordinary.
Eve. That's me. And this is my story.
No surname.
I used to carry my husband's.
But I came to hate him.
So I went back to my father's.
And then I came to hate him too.
So. No surname!
Oh, and don't take me for the stupid woman in the
    Bible story.
Who of course wasn't a real woman at all.
Just the invention of some misogynist priest.
My mum called me this because she liked the
    name.
My mum always took a fancy to the stupidest
    things.
Like my father.
So she called me Eve and all the boys used to
    shout after me
'E-eve. E-eve. Take your clothes off, Eve.'

SMITH   As an economist, ladies and gentlemen, I have to
    ask you: do you understand? Do you
    understand the forces that govern your lives?

HUME   Ladies and gentlemen, as a philosopher I am duty-
    bound to remind you:
 'Know yourself' was the dictum of the ancient
    Greeks.

EVE   And do we? Know ourselves?
               Let us use dialogue to discover!
               Ladies and gentlemen, the play begins!

               And so it does.

HUME   Mr Smith, my heart is beating!

SMITH   Mine too, Mr Hume. Hearts do tend to.

HUME   But what does it mean?

SMITH   The most likely hypothesis, Mr Hume, is that we
               are alive.

HUME   But that's impossible!

SMITH   Apparently not.

HUME   I have no business having a heart!
               And it has no business beating!

SMITH   But, Mr Hume. There it is.

HUME   Mr Smith, my last conscious memory was very
               distinctly of dying.
               There was not a shred of doubt about it!
               The fatal disease from which I was suffering had
               run its course.
               I was approaching my final dissolution.
               It was very disagreeable.

SMITH   I know. Horrible. It happened to me. I'm dead too.

HUME   The immensity of effort involved in dying!
               The strain of maintaining one's dignity and self-
               control in the face of all the assaults that are
               launched upon it...
               The intense discomfort. The humiliating
               weakness. The stabs of pain. The diarrhoea.
               The constant attacks of sheer animal terror.
               But I suffered it with every ounce of dignity,
               resolution and self-command.
               Christians had gathered round my moribund self
               like vultures.
               Eagerly seeking any sign of fear or weakness.
               But that was a satisfaction I denied them.

My dying, I can say in all modesty, was very
    creditable.
And I looked forward to its logical outcome:
The utter extinction of my conscious self.
But here I am. Alive!
Is all that labour to be in vain?
Am I to undergo the whole vile process again and
    again?
Furthermore, sir, as you know well, while I was
    still alive, in the period preceding my final
    dissolution,
I had proved, and proved with every recourse of
    reason, logic and wit,
The utter impossibility of life after death.
It was one of my finest essays.
Its structure was elegant, its reasoning irrefutable.
But here I am. Alive!
I can scarcely conceive the extent of my anger and
    dismay.
And how has this grotesque event come to be?
Who is responsible?
Silence.
Silence in the universe.
At least atheism is not disproved.
Silence in the dark and secret stars.
And that old fool Dante said they were moved by
    love.
Not love, Signor Dante. Physics! Moved by the
    laws of physics!
Unless that's another word for love.
But that is mere folly.

SMITH   Have some snuff.

HUME   Your equanimity amazes me.

SMITH   It is true, Mr Hume, that you argued with all your
    habitual eloquence and skill against the
    possibility of such an event. And that
    therefore this is not exactly the meeting we
    anticipated. But, my dear friend, life is a gift.
    Why not accept it? Have some snuff.

HUME   Oh, very well.

They take snuff. They sneeze.

We do appear still to be creatures of flesh and
    blood. That at least is some consolation.
It means that the ridiculous notion of the soul as a
    being separate from the body is exploded.
    Quite exploded. Another pinch?

They sneeze again.

It has always been perfectly clear to me that the
    notion of an immortal soul as distinct from a
    perishable body is a patent absurdity. Even
    the meanest intelligence should understand
    that the body and the soul are one!

SMITH   Precisely, Mr Hume. However, if you will forgive
    me for making this somewhat indelicate
    observation, our condition of corporeal
    resurrection would appear to vindicate St Paul.

HUME   Paul of Tarsus? That vile turncoat? That odious
    canting rogue?

SMITH   When he declared the doctrine of the resurrection
    of the flesh.

HUME   'The dead shall be raised incorruptible'?

SMITH   Precisely.

HUME   'O Death, where is thy sting? O Grave, where is
    thy victory?'

SMITH   Exactly. More snuff?

HUME   Of all the contemptible pieces of mendacity! Of
    all the disgraceful detestable abominable
    lying deceptions practised by the Christian
    Church!
Mr Smith, this is quite appalling! What shall we
    do?

SMITH   Were we in possession of claret, Mr Hume, I
    would suggest that we take it.

HUME   Claret, Mr Smith, is not sufficient!
              The thought that my existence in whatever sphere
                   I am now compelled to inhabit could possibly
                   be taken as confirmation of the despicable lies
                   of the Christian Church... This thought, Mr
                   Smith, distresses me so profoundly as to make
                   me quite lose my appetite.

SMITH   On the other hand, dear friend, I dare say things
                   could always be worse. Far worse.
              After all, my mother always said I would come to
                   a bad end.

HUME   Mr Smith, I fail to see the connection.

SMITH   'If you continue to associate with that wicked
                   atheistical Hume,' she said, 'Hell will be the
                   final resting place for the pair of you.'
              Perhaps she was right.

HUME   Mr Smith, your mother was an admirable woman.

SMITH   Admirable.

HUME   A woman of the rarest intelligence and sagacity.

SMITH   True, Mr Hume. Very true.

HUME   And yet when it came to matters of religion...

SMITH   She demonstrated the intelligence of a donkey and
                   the pertinacity of an ass. Also very true.
              Nonetheless I loved her dearly.

HUME   But, Mr Smith, we know that love is an admirable
                   sentiment.
              But love should never be allowed to get in the way
                   of the facts.

SMITH   But perhaps on this occasion...

HUME   Mr Smith, you cannot possibly be suggesting we
                   are in Hell.

SMITH   I will freely confess that as a hypothesis it is
                   somewhat improbable. Nonetheless, as
                   philosophers, we are duty-bound to entertain it.

HUME   Mr Smith, we have been led to believe that Hell is
            a place of indescribable horror.

SMITH   True.

HUME   And this place hardly qualifies.

SMITH   Also true.

HUME   I concede the space in which we find ourselves
            appears to have been built by persons totally
            lacking even the slightest traces of refinement
            and taste. I shudder to think of the
            characteristics of the age capable of
            committing such an outrage to the aesthetic
            sense.
            However: you must concede, Mr Smith, it does not
            correspond to any known definition of Hell.

SMITH   I do concede, Mr Hume.
            And its denizens do not appear to be souls in
            torment.

HUME   Absolutely not, Mr Smith.

SMITH   Instead I would describe them as fat. Very fat.

HUME   Fat, Mr Smith?

SMITH   Perhaps I am guilty of a certain exaggeration. But
            at least prosperous. Sleek.

HUME   Mr Smith, you are correct. They are sleek. Almost
            greasy. More so than the average. Or at least
            the average to which we are accustomed.
            Furthermore, their skin is not pockmarked, nor
            their bodies conspicuously deformed.
            Nor do they smell. They appear to wash with
            remarkable regularity. The stink of human
            ordure is conspicuously absent.

SMITH   Mr Hume, an idea is forming. The inhabitants of
            this place... Their obvious prosperity... Their
            cleanliness and apparent health.
            Is it possible, Mr Hume... Dare I imagine...

HUME   Imagine what, Mr Smith?

SMITH   That the world could have changed?
That we could have stumbled across an age where
markets are actually allowed to operate freely?
Where human affairs are actually governed by the
wisdom of the market's hidden hand?
That the state of affairs we dreamt of and worked
to bring about could actually have come into
being?

HUME   And that we could have entered a world...

SMITH   A world governed by reason.

HUME   Where people's creative energies have been set
free by commerce...

SMITH   ...Commerce untrammelled by regulation and
monopoly...

HUME   A world where the sick perverted absurdities of
organised religion no longer hold sway...

SMITH   A happy world...

HUME   A world of order and justice...

SMITH   A world ruled by enlightened philosophy.
Paradise, Mr Hume.

HUME   The earthly paradise.

SMITH   Philosophy admitting of no other kind.

HUME   Mr Smith...

SMITH   Mr Hume...

HUME   Is it possible that people actually read our books?

SMITH   And then took notice of them?

HUME   It seems scarcely plausible.

SMITH   Given the chronic disorder of human affairs.

HUME   Nonetheless, Mr Smith...

SMITH   Mr Hume?

HUME   The hypothesis is distinctly enticing.

SMITH   Then let us embrace it.

HUME   In which case, Mr Smith, it is no longer a question
          of our being in Hell.

SMITH   Rather that we are in Heaven.

HUME   Snuff, Mr Smith?

SMITH   Delighted, Mr Hume.

          They take snuff. They sneeze.

HUME   How wonderful an opportunity this is, Mr Smith,
          to exercise our reason in the operations of
          philosophy.

SMITH   Reason is one thing, Mr Hume. The market is
          another.
          I know we hypothesised that if the market were
          allowed free scope for its operations it would
          have an improving effect on human affairs.

HUME   And how fascinating to be able to observe it.

SMITH   But I do not intend merely to observe it. I spent a
          lifetime, Mr Hume, a whole weary lifetime,
          observing the market.
          A whole lifetime observing: because I was too
          frightened to live.
          That I intend to remedy.

HUME   Mr Smith, you alarm me. Your mother...

SMITH   ...would not approve, Mr Hume.
          Would definitely undoubtedly and categorically
          not approve.

HUME   Your mother was an admirable woman.

SMITH   Admirable. Undoubtedly.
          But also tyrannical. Judgemental. Intolerable!
          She was a woman, Hume, in whom Christianity,
          the curse of our dismal country, Christianity, I
          say, a woman in whom Christianity in all its
          dreadful aspects was profoundly rooted. And
          which then came into full, bitter flower in the

course of a hidebound duty-dominated
existence!

A woman whose whole being was governed by the
sour, bitter, damnable life-denying spirit of
John Knox!

A woman obsessed with the fear of happiness and
dominated by the dread of pleasure! A dread
she thoroughly implanted in me!

Implanted in me all the more damnably because I
so devotedly loved her.

I mourned her passing in the deepest grief

And for what remained of my life tried to be
worthy of her memory.

Like you I have a memory, Hume, of dying.

Like yours my death was a prolonged affair.

My stomach would not admit digestion.

And as I slowly wasted my mind was much taken
up with regrets:

Of the imperfections in the books I had completed

Of the books I had left unwritten

Of the life I had not led.

The cities I had left unvisited.

The vices I had never explored.

The men I had not kissed.

HUME	Men, Mr Smith?
SMITH	Of course.
HUME	But we were always such good friends!
SMITH	And, Mr Hume?
HUME	Does that mean...?
SMITH	I include you in the category of men I have not kissed? Of course it does.
HUME	You never showed the slightest inclination!
SMITH	How could I, Mr Hume? Does that surprise you? Of course we never spoke of such things. We could not, Hume, ever speak of such things.

Did it not occur to you that my timidity and
    shyness might have had some hidden cause?
Or there might be some secret reason for my
    obsessive concern with self-command?
The fact that such things were left unspoken,
    Hume, did not make them any less urgent.
Did not make them any less real.
I tried my utmost to ignore them and was, on the
    whole, successful.
But my success in this regard did not render less
    piercing my regret.
But today, Hume, today when by some miracle I
    again find myself in possession of my physical
    faculties and the full ability to enjoy them –
    and with not a mother in sight – well, my
    member goes erect at the very thought of them!

HUME   So what are you going to do?

SMITH   Freedom beckons, Hume. I intend to follow her
    call.

HUME   But, Mr Smith, we cannot simply allow ourselves
    to be carried away by our passions.

SMITH   I can.

HUME   But what of reason?
    What of self-command?
    What of the impartial spectator?

SMITH   I trample them into the dust.
    Join me.

HUME   Never.

SMITH   You want to.
    I know you secretly want to.

HUME   I most certainly do not.

SMITH   Very well. I shall join a club.

HUME   A club?

SMITH   Not a philosophical society or the select society or
    any of the endless insipid dull societies that

we attempted to found and then so tiresomely
joined to improve the common weal but a
drinking club!
A club devoted to the pleasures of the flesh!
The hellfire club! The sweating club! The quart-
of-claret club! The gallon-of-claret club!
Clubs whose purpose are so depraved we can
barely even conceive of them! The Molly
House, Hume. The Molly House. Freedom,
Hume! Freedom! Freedom!

Exit ADAM SMITH.

HUME I am a reasonable man.
I know the strength of the passions and I take this
  into account.
And I will not let them dominate my actions
Or overpower me in my mind.
Nonetheless.
This
Is
An
Outrage.
AN OUTRAGE!
How dare he leave me like this!
How dare he!

EVE Mr Hume, calm down.

HUME Calm down. Calm down!
When words can barely conceive the depths of my
  outrage and dismay?

EVE Yes. Calm down. Be enlightened.

HUME Enlightened! What's the use of being enlightened?

EVE You disappoint me.

HUME Madam, you must admit the provocation is
  considerable.

EVE Of course, Mr Hume. But pause a moment.
As a fervent admirer, I beg you to reflect.
Remember: there was a woman who'd just had
  supper in your new town house

And wrote with chalk on the wall opposite your
    new front door:
'St David's Street' because she thought you a
    good man. She thought you were a saint. I
    like that story.
Don't let me down, Mr Hume.
I have met very few good men in my life and I
    want you to be one of them.
Is this the behaviour of a saint?

HUME   Most saints I have read of, madam, are the
    stupidest, most egoistical creatures on this
    Earth. If there was a God I would give him
    thanks for not making me one of them. As it
    is, madam...
Let me assure you I am no saint.
I simply endeavour to be a decent human being.
And I do remember. I remember that lady. Nancy
    Ord. We had an especially fine meal that
    night. The *Soupe à la Reine* whose recipe I
    brought back from France. And I also
    remember. Madam, I swear it is as if I can see
    it before my very eyes. There. The declivity
    between the old town of Edinburgh and the
    new. And it is the most pestilential bog. All
    the excrement from the town flows into it. I
    am walking from my old town house to
    inspect the workings on the new and I have
    the misfortune to lose my footing and fall into
    it up to my waist. And I can not extricate
    myself. I am a most pitiful object. And an old
    woman who happens to be passing, a
    churchgoer, sees me in this state. And, me
    being known for a notorious atheist, will not
    pull me out until I say the Lord's Prayer. A
    saint, madam, would have allowed himself to
    sink into the shit and drown. As it was, I can
    repeat the Lord's Prayer without a qualm.
    Forgive us our trespasses, madam.

EVE   As we forgive them who trespass against us.

HUME   Precisely.

EVE   And she pulls you out the bog, and you have a
          wee chat, and you say she is an excellent
          natural theologian and she says you are a
          good Christian soul after all.

HUME   Madam, you are remarkably well informed.

EVE   The strange thing is, Mr Hume, we belong to such
          different worlds.
          We speak different.
          And there's you in your beautiful new town house.
          Which I can see. See so clearly in the eye of my
          mind.
          So elegant. So beautiful.
          Me, I lived in Glenrothes.
          That was a new town too, I suppose.
          But rather different.
          And you were learned, and I was ignorant.
          And you were a man, and I was a woman.
          The one thing we have in common is that we're
          both dead.
          Only you died slow, and thought about it,
          And I died fast, and didn't.
          Heart attack, Mr Hume. Overwhelming.
          Like a giant wave and a fragmentation bomb.
          Both at once.
          Scattering. Obliterating.
          And you're right.
          Atrociously disagreeable.
          And then a long time in a dreary desert
          Searching for the fragments
          Putting them in a jar
          Trying to put them all together again.
          Lucky I always loved jigsaws.
          I think you're a piece in the right-hand corner
          somewhere.
          Do you understand?

HUME   Madam, I am endeavouring to do so.

EVE   My guess is, Mr Hume, is that being so
          exceptionally strong-minded a person in life...

HUME   Madam, you honour me.

EVE   … And being so utterly determined that there was
                no life after death, you did in fact extinguish
                your existence for some considerable time.
                The theory being, Mr Hume, that life here is the
                creation of our previous state of mind.

HUME   Madam, it is a hypothesis I shall endeavour to
                entertain.

EVE   Your turn, Mr Hume. Your turn to honour me.

HUME   And may I ask how you came by this remarkable
                theory, madam?

EVE   Having put myself together again, Mr Hume, and
                having admired the result, I started to look
                about me. And found myself in the company
                of a venerable gentleman reading aloud to a
                dead person in a coffin. To the
                accompaniment of gentle gongs. You don't
                happen to read Tibetan?

HUME   Madam, that is an accomplishment that I regret I
                lack.

EVE   Me too, Mr Hume. But I knew it was Tibetan.
                Ancient Tibetan. And I knew I understood it.

HUME   The hypothesis being that the human mind
                possesses gifts we are utterly unaware of?

EVE   Precisely, Mr Hume. Which is what enables the
                likes of me to have a conversation with the
                likes of you.

HUME   Or vice versa.

EVE   Exactly. And the book the gentleman was reading
                were instructions to the recently deceased. To
                tell them how to conduct themselves in the
                afterlife. It was *The Tibetan Book of the Dead*,
                Mr Hume. *The Tibetan Book of the Dead*! It
                being a book my mum picked up at a jumble
                sale and never read. It being incomprehensible
                at the time. And that my dad then tore the
                pages out of to light his fags with.

HUME   Madam, my senses tell me we are speaking
          together.
          But I must confess I find it hard to give credit to
          them.

EVE   You used to worry, Mr Hume, about whether we
          were correct to trust the evidence of our
          senses.
          To assume the Sun really would rise each morning
          or that the world would stay the same.
          Whether the table would stay a table or the chair a
          chair
          Or this theatre remain a theatre.

HUME   I did have such concerns. It's true. They frightened
          me. I thought I might end up a prisoner in
          Bedlam to be whipped and chained.
          And displayed as an exhibit of fear and derision.

EVE   You were courageous, Mr Hume. And you were
          wise.
          You said that in the end the human mind was
          predisposed to believe our senses and that in
          fact we have to do so or life becomes
          impossible. And so we do it, and we believe
          this chair will stay a chair and that the Sun will
          rise again tomorrow morning, but never quite
          closing ourselves to the possibility that we may
          be wrong. Staying alert. Enquiring. Sceptical.

HUME   Madam, I am deeply flattered by the interest that
          you show in me.

EVE   Imagine me, Mr Hume. In London. In the catering
          trade.
          Working twelve, fourteen hours a day.
          Successful. Making a heap of money.
          But totally ignorant.
          I can do silver service with a blindfold on
          And find I have a passion for training other people
          to do it. But I know nothing about the world
          at all. And there I am on the Tube. Hurtling
          from one job to the next down a stinking dark
          tunnel. Wondering why.

And then I see a poster.
'Discover the Meaning of Life.
Do a course in philosophy.'
And I think: meaning in life. I could do with some
   of that.
And twenty years later, after selling my business
   and with nothing better to do, that's exactly
   what I do.
Go to night school to study philosophy.
I don't think I discover the meaning of life, Mr
   Hume, but I do discover you. You and your
   friend.
You were probably the last activity of my conscious
   mind. Perhaps that's why I've met you.
The Tibetan theory being, Mr Hume, is that this all
   functions like a dream.

HUME   Some philosophers said life was just a dream.
            I never had any time for it.

EVE   My mum used to say that.

HUME   I meant your mother no disrespect.

EVE   Say it in the bad times.
            This whole life's a dream, she'd say, beaten up, the
               blood running down her, and one day we'll all
               wake up. All wake up from this fucking mess
               and everything'll be just fine. That's what
               she'd say. Bruised and bleeding and
               everything. My mum. Always reading books.
               Not that there were that many books in
               Glenrothes. She'd pick them up from dustbins
               or jumble sales or places and bring them home.
               And then she'd be reading them. She read once
               about a Chinese philosopher dreamt he was a
               butterfly. And then didn't know if he was a
               man dreaming he was a butterfly or a butterfly
               dreaming he was a man. Friend of yours?

HUME   I regret we never met. Because seen from this
               perspective, it seems it may be true. I feel as
               though I truly was. Dreaming. My life. My
               books. Everything.

EVE   She never had anywhere to put them. All her
            books. So they just lay about in heaps
            everywhere. And when it got really cold and
            we had nothing else we'd burn them. Books
            burn really badly, Mr Hume.

HUME   I believe they are sold for reading.
            Indeed that was the basis of my livelihood.
            I made considerable sums.
            I built myself a very fine town house.
            This house. This house of which I am so proud.
            This elegant expression of the capacities of the
            human mind.

EVE   It's beautiful, Mr Hume.
            As I would expect. I was proud of my house too.
            I lived in a new town too.
            But Glenrothes isn't quite like this.
            And you paid for yours through writing.
            I paid for mine through working.
            Oh look. I can show you how I paid for it.
            Put this on.

HUME   What is this?

EVE   A uniform.

HUME   I wore a uniform once. I detested it.
            I was secretary to a general.
            We were ordered to invade Canada. But we got no
                further than the Isle of Wight. It was felt that
                we should still do something and so were
                ordered to invade France. So we set off for
                France with our highly skilled contingent of
                Indian guides. But no maps of France. Military
                organisation is neither rational nor effective.
                The folly I witnessed in the army, madam, was
                so colossal no satirist could invent it.

EVE   We're not in the army, Mr Hume. I promise.
            We're at General Instruments Microelectronics
                Test Department, in Silicon Glen. Eastfield
                Industrial Estate, Glenrothes.
            Now put this on.

It's 1976 or thereabouts,
and the factory assembles silicon chips.
And they're a...
They're a kind of model of the human brain.
Only better.
They can calculate faster
They can take over so much drudgery and routine
stuff
And it means the working week is going to be so
much shorter
And we're going to have so much leisure
And then we'll have so much time to play these
games!
Look, Mr Hume. This is the game.
It's called Pong.
You each have a bat and you knock the ball from
one end of the screen to the other.

They play the game on the screen a moment.

Isn't it fun?

HUME   Forgive me for saying so, madam, but this is but a
crude device.

EVE   No, Mr Hume. You don't understand.
These games are so amazing and they are the
future, Mr Hume!
Everyone wants them.
I love this job.
I love this uniform. It's so white.
It's like you were a surgeon or something.
It's so clean!
I love the fact they pay you to keep clean!
The last job I had was so dirty!
I worked in a golf-bag factory.
It was mingin.
And they only paid eighteen pound a week.
This job pays forty-five.
And forty-five pounds a week is such good money!
And I can save up to get married
And save up to get a deposit on a house.
And it's more than that

It's modern! It's the future!

These are computer chips!

Don't ask me, Mr Hume. I don't really
understand.

I don't need to.

It's good money, Mr Hume. Good money!

They're all put together in other bits of the factory
and this is where we check them, see?

In the test area. This is the test area.

So don't just stand there, Mr Hume.

Put on the uniform.

We have to cover ourselves up and we have to put
on the face mask, because this place has to be
so clean, it has to be cleaner than an operating
theatre, and I hook up my pinky to the wire so
I'm earthed, in case I frizzle up or something,
and now we start.

Ready?

So I begin:

You take the device.

The device. That's what this is. This. The device.

You take the device and you check its legs.

You'll see it has five legs and they all have to be
straight. See. Five legs. See? Five legs!

And this one's not straight.

So I take out my long-nosed pliers.

And you take out yours.

Your long-nosed pliers! From your overall pocket.
Your pliers! Not your tweezers!

So you take your pliers.

Your long-nosed pliers.

And you straighten the leg.

See. Like this. And then you put it in the test
socket.

Like this.

North south east west check all the corners.

Ping pong ping pong. Hear that, Mr Hume?

It means it's correct. So you put it in the accept bin.

The accept bin, Mr Hume!

Then you take another. You check its legs. You put
it in the test socket. North south east west

check. Ping pong ping pong. North south east
west check all the corners.
If it's correct put it in the accept bin.
If it's faulty put it in the reject bin.
The whole procedure should take five seconds.
Which means you do twelve every minute.
Seven hundred and twenty an hour.
Five thousand seven hundred and sixty in the
working day. Twenty-eight thousand eight
hundred in the working week. One million
four hundred and forty thousand a year. With
two weeks holiday. That's your quota.
And if you meet your quota, you get on. Which I
intend to do.
I'm saving up for my wedding.

HUME   Madam, I admire your industry.

EVE   I've done six and you've hardly done any!
You had to take an entrance test to get in.
I loved the test!
There was long division and everything.
You'd have failed it.

HUME   Madam, the general principles of this activity are
familiar to me.
Mr Smith and I, we analysed it in the context of
pins.
I can understand pins.

EVE   Don't worry, Mr Hume, no one understands this.
No one anywhere at all.
Like I said, no one needs to.
Don't get upset. Tell me about pins.

HUME   We can divide the manufacture of pins
Into about eighteen different operations.
One man draws out the wire, another straights it,
another points it, a fifth grinds it at the top for
receiving the head...
Let us assume a small manufactury where ten men
are employed. If they exert themselves they
can make among them about twelve pounds
of pins in a day. And in a pound there are at

least twelve thousand pins of a middling size.
We are talking therefore of forty-eight
thousand pins. Being produced in a day.
Whereas had the same men been working
individually they could not have made more
than twenty.
And the surplus generated by the difference
between what a man can produce individually
and what he can produce collectively...
It is that surplus, madam, which is invariably
considerable, that surplus which is
transforming the world.

EVE   Mine as well as yours.

HUME   And it arises from the fact that we have learnt to
work together collectively. A better way.
Not in the destructive and absurd business of
making war, but in the constructive and
creative business of the market.
However, madam, to analyse it theoretically is one
thing.
To be actively engaged in it is quite another.
I do not consider this an activity fit for human
beings.
I shall therefore desist.

EVE   But you can't stop, Mr Hume.
None of us can afford to stop.

HUME   The iron law of necessity still prevails?

EVE   We have to earn a living.

HUME   So certain fundamentals have not changed.
But given that, madam, surely you can occupy
yourself more gainfully than this. You have a
keen mind.
Why don't you study?

EVE   You mean why not go to college?
I can't go to college
Because my dad says we can't afford it.
And we can't afford it because my dad spends all
his wages on booze,

And Mum keeps giving money to the
    Scientologists so she can be a thetan, and that
    means often we just don't have any food in
    the house.
And I know I love long division and those
    beautiful chemical formulas
And I'm very good at netball and everything
But what's the point of it?
What's the point of it when there's no one caring?
And with a wage I can put food on the table
And we don't have to eat Mum's burnt chips
And pretend to like them
So she doesn't go mad and throw the plates
    everywhere.
For the first time in my life, Mr Hume,
There's food on the table
And no one goes hungry.
And that's why
That's why I don't go to college.

HUME   Madam, there must be something better you can
       do!

EVE   But everyone does this, Mr Hume.
       Everyone works at jobs they detest and that don't
           employ their full capacities.
       And we earn wages to spend money on goods that
           have been made by fellow humans in the
           same kinds of jobs who earn money so they
           can spend it. And so the world goes round, Mr
           Hume.

HUME   We thought it would progress.

EVE   And it has. I've got a good job. People envy me.
       And I'm saving up to buy a house.
       Look, this is the kitchen.

HUME   This is a kitchen?

EVE   It's beautiful. It's fitted. We never had a fitted
       kitchen. Look, it's got cupboards.
       We never had cupboards.

HUME   Very creditable, I'm sure.

EVE   And this is the living room. Look at the curtains!
           Red roses. With the valance and everything. I
           always wanted a valance. We never had
           curtains.

HUME   Is not it all somewhat cramped?

EVE   Not at all. This is a good-size house.
           This is spacious. Compared to Glasgow this is
           spacious.
           That's where I was born, Mr Hume.
           Five of us in the one room. And sharing a toilet
           with five families on the stair. No trees, no
           grass, nothing. You see the park across the
           road? Trees, Mr Hume. Grass. Flowers! And
           we can go there. We can go there and play.
           For a young child, Mr Hume, a young child
           brought up in squalor, this is paradise.

HUME   I try to feel enthusiasm for your achievements,
           madam, but I find it hard.
           Madam, I do not wish to boast but my house has a
           sense of beauty and proportionality this
           dwelling entirely lacks.
           Beauty matters, madam.
           There is a lack of aesthetic value in your house
           that fills me with dismay.

EVE   But we don't do aesthetic value here, Mr Hume.
           This is Glenrothes.

HUME   And this is how you live?

EVE   This is how we live.
           And we're so lucky, Mr Hume.
           Compared to how we used to live.

HUME   And all these people, madam,
           These humans who labour in their millions
           That the market imprisons in drudgery
           How do they take their pleasure?

           Enter SMITH.

SMITH   Itchi witchi weeza
           Itchi witchi weeza

              BOOM ba ba BOOM
              Ba ba BOOM BOOM BOOM.

EVE   Like this, Mr Hume.
              Just like this.

SMITH   Claret, Humey, claret is history!
              Techno rules!

HUME   Mr Smith, collect yourself

SMITH   No no, Humey, not collect myself not collect
                  myself!
              Lose myself, Humey. Lose. Myself.
              Lose myself in the music!
              In the beat, Humey. New word. Beat. In. The. Beat.

HUME   I lament the downfall of one of the greatest minds
                  of Europe.

EVE   Don't worry, Mr Hume. There's stuff all over the
                  clubs.
              He's just been given something.
              Ecstasy maybe. Or ketamine. A horse tranquilliser.

HUME   Horse tranquilliser?

EVE   They say, Mr Hume, it gives the intensest
                  pleasure. Don't fret.
              He'll get over it.

SMITH   Found a club, Humey, found the most stupendous
                  club!
              Not quite what I expected
              But stupendous.
              Stu stu stu stu stu. Pend. Ous.
              Water. Water water water water give me water.
              Noisy place. Very.
               Wotcha wotcha wotcha
              Lights. Lights lights lights lights!
              Beating beating in time with music
              How did they do that?
              Didn't like it at first
              But they gave me something
              Little pill

You can buy it on the market
Buy ecstasy on the market, Hume
It is wonderful
Took the pill
Water water lots of water
And something happened
Watcha boom watcha boom
Watcha BOOM BOOM BOOM
And and and and and and
I lost myself
Mr Hume Mr Hume Mr Hume
Losing yourself is the most amazing sensation
The impartial spectator just closes his eyes
And you can crumple him up
And put him in your mouth and eat him!
And he's gone!
Like a huge burden
Fallen off my shoulders
And I saw I saw the moment
The moment was greeny blue
And I saw the invisible hand
Beaming beneficentlylylyly
Eezy weezy boom! Eezy weezy boom!
Hume my friend Humey booms
Eezy weezy eezy weezy
And the dancing, Humey.
The dancing.

EVE   Stop dancing, Mr Smith, you'll do yourself an
           injury.

SMITH   Eeeji weeji.

EVE   Stop it, Mr Smith! This minute!
           Now sit down. There's a good boy.

SMITH   But what will Mother say?

EVE   Don't worry, Mr Smith. We won't tell her.

SMITH   She'd be worried if she knew.

EVE   Now you mustn't get cold, Mr Smith. Let me tuck
           you in.

SMITH   I'll tell her I've been out researching.

EVE   And so you have, Mr Smith. So you have.
Now cuddle down.

HUME   His 'Theory of Moral Sentiments' was the finest
thing.

EVE   Don't worry, Mr Hume. When he wakes up he'll
be himself again.

HUME   Madam, I am eternally in your debt.
But forgive me for asking.
Is this how you always dance?

EVE   I remember dancing, Mr Hume.
I'm dancing at my wedding.
Everyone is. Everyone's dancing.
Everyone keeps wanting me to dance and I don't
want to
But I must.
My dress is so huge
And so tight in the waist
It is imprisoning me
My dad's spent a fortune
Money he doesn't have
And my brother starts fighting with his brother
And the two mums start screaming at each other
And I feel so ashamed I could die
I hate it
I hate all of it
All I want to do is sleep.
But they won't let me
And I don't want to have it that night
Not in the big four-poster bed
Which I know my dad can't really pay for.

HUME   Does nothing ever really change?

SMITH   I feel so ill.

HUME   Self-command, Mr Smith. Remember self-
command.

SMITH   But life is so much more pleasant without it!
And the market operates so much better without it.

Reason restricts life, Humey. The market expands it. Take the pill, Humey. Take the pill. Ecstasy can be bought and sold. I understand it is illegal, but that is a detail. A piffling detail! It will become freely available. Ecstasy, Humey! That was once the preserve of mystics and saints! The market will prevail!

SMITH *vomits*.

There. I feel better already.
Now, Humey, I must show you this.

HUME I wish you would not address me with that vulgar term.
And call me old fashioned, but I also wish, Mr Smith, you would use the honorific.
Its absence unsettles me.

SMITH What is he talking about?

HUME I can scarcely believe the extent of your degeneration.
Good manners, Mr Smith, not to mention the most basic demands of mutual respect, demand that we address each other as 'mister'.

SMITH Good manners are finished, Humey.
In this world they don't exist.
What we have instead is this.

HUME And what is that?
Oh, don't answer.
For once I despair of dialogue!
I will tell you what it is, Mr Smith, it is a shiny little box.
It signifies nothing!
Like everything in your farrago!
This torrent of nonsense that you have vomited all over us!
Have the good manners to be silent!

SMITH May I first remark in passing, Humey, that for one renowned for his affability and moderation,

you have become quite astonishingly bad
tempered.

HUME   And have I not just cause?

SMITH   Is it so terrible to discover that everything you
dreamed of has come into being?
You dreamed of a society where reason would
flourish unfettered by religion. Unfettered by
prejudice and superstition. And this is what
has come about. They have broken everything
down, Humey, broken everything down into
its component parts and this is what they have
come up with. This is one of the marvels,
Humey, one of the marvels they have come
up with. In three hundred short years they
have created marvels that we were incapable
of even conceiving!
This shiny little box, Humey, that you so despise
is being produced in its millions. Every single
one of them sitting here can have one! And in
a few years' time, Humey, they will be
available to every single person in the world!
And let me tell you what it does, Humey. Let me
just tell you.
Remember the mail, Humey? Remember how
slow it was, how hopelessly unreliable?
With this I can talk with anyone anywhere.
I can write a message to anyone in the world and
they will get it the very instant I send it.
Remember sitting for your portrait, Humey?
Remember how long it took?
I can point this at you and make you a portrait this
very instant! Here! And here! And here!
I can reproduce you walking, I can reproduce you
sitting, I can reproduce you sighing, I can
reproduce your every gesture! Whether of joy,
of anger, of wonderment or despair! And I can
send it to anyone I want to. Anyone in the
whole wide world! Remember those old
portraits, Humey? Remember how stupid you
always looked? How bovine? How glazed your

expression was? You used to look like that to
disguise the thoughts that were boiling in your
brain! Look how good you were! Only perhaps
you've really become stupid! Stupid because
you won't recognise the consequences of what
you have done! And the consequences, Humey,
baffle the mind and confound the imagination!
Because this little box, Humey, is a device
which connects! Connects with everyone and
everything! Connects in the present and
connects through time! It is a repository,
Humey, an immense storehouse of all the
information that exists in the world!
Remember the labour, Humey, the immense
labour we had to undergo to gather even the
most insignificant details? The struggle you
had to gain access to a library of books?
It's all over!
These people have access to every piece of
information they will ever need!
It's there. In their hands. They carry it around with
them in their pockets and in their bag.
This is power, Humey!
Power we could not even begin to imagine!
But one thing we did get right.
Because all this has come about not through the
Church, not through royalty, not the
aristocracy.
Not through the army or the use of force.
But through the free operation of the market.
Hear that, Humey? The market has done this!
The market has set free the creative power of
human ingenuity!
And they all have it! They all have it in their
hands!
Of course they don't know what they want to do
with it. They peddle gossip. They buy their
groceries. Or they get the weather forecast.
But they'll learn, Humey. They'll soon learn.
Revolutions, Humey. Revolutions will be born
from this!

As for me, what will I do with it?
What do you think?
I could look up the works of Plato.
Or of yourself.
One of your followers has assembled your works
    in the most elegant and accessible manner.
I could even read my own.
But why would I want to read of the wealth of
    nations when I can so easily enjoy it?
I suppose I could peruse the works of the greatest
    sages the world has ever known.
But I prefer to use it to find a young person willing
    to indulge me in a spot of anal intercourse.
Now don't talk to me.
I need to concentrate.

Silence.

HUME   I despair of my dear friend.
            First he is degenerated by some chemical
                substance.
            And now this.
            Enslaved by the body's grossest passions.
            Madam, tell me, can what he talks of possibly be
                true?
            Can these monstrous wonders really exist?

EVE   They can, Mr Hume. They do.
            What we witnessed in my factory was the start of
                it.
            It's all happened faster than anyone could
                imagine.

HUME   It is true what he said about books.
            It was only with the greatest of difficulty that I
                could obtain the books I required.
            But can it really be possible for every book to be
                available?
            Every book in the world?

SMITH   Height: six foot.
            Muscled? Oh yes.
            Eyes? Blue.
            Hair? Hair? Can I ask for a wig?

EVE   Of course you can, Mr Smith.
            You can ask for anything.

SMITH   Anything?

EVE   Anything.

HUME   When books had to be written by hand, the church
                could limit access to the truth.
            They were afraid of it because it would expose
                their lies. They were even afraid of people
                reading the Bible itself! But that ended with
                the invention of the printing press. And that
                changed everything.

SMITH   Do I want top or bottom?
            What do you think?

EVE   Say both.

SMITH   Am I well hung?

EVE   Say yes.

SMITH   Water sports?

EVE   No.

HUME   Historians tend to think of history as to do with
                famous people. I know. I used to be one. With
                kings or with queens or statesmen or famous
                generals. With events. But they just cause
                disturbance on the surface of things. It is not
                events: it is through ideas that the world is
                changed.

EVE   I have lived through this.
            They are living through it now.
            You spoke of Caxton and the printing press and
                how it changed everything. As a historian you
                would know such things. But the change this
                represents is something greater still.

SMITH   Rimming?

EVE   I would say yes. Very much to my surprise.

HUME   But how can books be put into so small a
                machine?

EVE   You know, Mr Hume, you can turn letters into numbers. By a kind of code. I had this maths teacher and we did them at school. Got us all mad about them. And then once you have them into numbers, you can turn them into binary numbers. We weren't meant to but we did. Means you can break everything down into ones and zeroes.

SMITH   Bears? I never said anything about animals.

EVE   It means beards. Do you like men with beards?

SMITH   So it is a typographical error?

HUME   Leibniz. He wrote of this. It came down to him from the Chinese. I always imagined it to be so much useless speculation.

EVE   But that's how it all works. Through electricity. On or off. One or zero. Yes or no.

SMITH   Enough questions! Time for action!
          See, Humey?
          This is a new form of writing. It's called typing. See how I master it? And then I press send.

HUME   But the binary system transforms even the simplest numbers into numbers of the most enormous length! That's why I disregarded it.

EVE   Don't ask me how, Mr Hume, because I don't understand. But those circuits I was making mean the operation can be completed at unimaginable speeds.

SMITH   Oh my God there is a man in the bar!
          And he wants me!
          Look, Humey. Look how handsome he is!
          And this extraordinary man is waiting for me at the top of these stairs!
          It's a miracle! This is paradise!
          And we made it happen, Humey!
          We made it happen!
          We are great people now!

You have a statue on the High Street!
Did you know that? Outside the law courts.
You're wearing a toga!
You look ridiculous!
I've got a statue too.
Mine's bigger.
I'm carrying wheatsheaves!
I look majestic. Commanding!
And now. If you'll forgive me.
I will go and get buggered.

Exit SMITH.

HUME   Madam, I cannot understand it.
                While he lived, he never showed the slightest sign
                    of any such rampant inclination to vice. He
                    was always so shy with women. All women
                    that is, except his mother.
                On the other hand, I preferred the company of
                    women. All women. All women except his
                    mother. Provided they were witty, they were
                    intelligent, and they were chaste. Like
                    yourself, madam.

EVE   I'm not sure I was ever very chaste.

HUME   Early experiments persuaded me that conventional
                    domestic life was not for me.
                I too greatly valued my freedom.
                And I would never have made an adequate
                    husband. Still less a good father. The demands
                    of my first love, writing, were far too great.
                And my physical needs were mercifully slight.
                In this, as in all things, I was most fortunate.
                My dear friend less so. It's true he has
                    disappointed me somewhat, but I will not
                    follow the path of the canting Christians and
                    condemn him.
                For who are we to judge?
                Even if we were to try to obey the rantings of
                    Yahweh, that old despot, and try to find ten
                    good men to save from the city of Sodom.
                    Find ten good men we could save from

destruction, could we do it? Could we find ten good men here? In this assembly? Ten men in whom the usual mixture of good and evil firmly and unequivocally comes down on the side of good?
Madam?

EVE   Those things my husband does to me
           Mostly I don't really like what he does to me
           I think perhaps I should and I worry there's
               something wrong with me
           I don't want to be a lesbian or something
           So I try to like it.
           And usually I don't tell him when I don't.
           My mum never liked it.
           'Some things you just have to put up with,' she
               says.
           'Men need to do them.'
           I hate it in the mornings
           He just rolls over on top of me with his hard-on
           As if I were a dishrag or something
           A rag he wipes his penis with.
           And it's like that tonight
           The night of my wedding
           And I say please no
           But he pins me down
           He says don't be ridiculous
           And it hurts
           It hurts more than ever.
           'Can't have the boys at work laugh at me'
           He says
           'Can't have them laugh at me
           Because I haven't banged you up.'
           What does reason say, Mr Hume?
           What does reason say to this?

HUME   Reasons tells your husband to reflect.

EVE   And what if he doesn't listen?

HUME   Reason says: stop a moment. Think!
           Is the approbation of your workmates really more
               important than the happiness of your wife?

  Understand for the sake of your own happiness
    also, that love between husband and wife
    should be a mutually pleasurable act.

EVE He isn't listening.

HUME Madam, I never claimed reason on its own is
    always sufficient!

EVE It never is, Mr Hume. It never is!

HUME You do me an injustice. Perhaps it cannot prevent
    human suffering. But sometimes it can
    mitigate its effects.

EVE I fall pregnant, Mr Hume.
  I am carrying new life inside me
  And the father is a man I perhaps once thought I
    loved
  But who now I find repugnant.
  I do not want to carry his child.

HUME Reason would tell you to have the child removed.

EVE Reason is quite correct, Mr Hume.

HUME Was this not attended by great danger?
  In my time squalid women practised this in dirty
    rooms.

EVE Not now, Mr Hume.
  Now I can go to a doctor and it is in safety these
    things can be performed.
  Freely and safely. Things have changed.
  And were your friend here I would tell him:
  This has nothing to do with the market.
  Nothing to do with anyone's desire to enrich
    themselves.
  Not the market, Mr Hume. The National Health
    Service.
  The result of an aspiration to build a better
    world.

HUME That is part of what reason is for.
  So we can understand.
  Understand better and improve.

EVE   I reasoned, Mr Hume. I went to the doctor.
I told him what had happened.
I told him my husband had raped me and I could
    not bear to carry the child.
I was lucky, Mr Hume, lucky to find one who
    listened.
He made me an appointment
And I went.
And I'm in the waiting room.
It is somewhere safe and clean, I can tell that,
    but...
I am sitting in a chair, one of those plastic ones
    that can be wiped clean,
And suddenly I feel
I feel new life inside me
New life stirring
New life waiting to be born.
I can't bear it
I cannot bear to have it scooped out of me.
I go to the woman at the desk
I say
'I'm sorry'
And I go home.

HUME   Perhaps in someone like yourself, madam,
    someone who so deeply loves life, perhaps
    the instinct for life will always somehow
    prevail.

EVE   But I'm still reasoning, Mr Hume.
I think if I am to keep this child
It will need a father.
So I think:
Home is where my husband is.
So I go back to him.
He's left the house go squalid
But I clean it up again.
I try to be nice.
I try to be reconciled
We live together for a while,
With the new life, the new life growing all the
    time inside me,

Living in that same house of which I was once so
    proud
But which now seems cramped and dangerous and
    mean.
He always comes home late.
He's working extra shifts, he says.
Letters start coming through the door
And when I ask him what they are he starts to
    shout
And I shout back
And then he hits me
And I go upstairs to pack my things
And he comes after me and shouts
'Good riddance, bitch!'
And throws me down the stairs.

Pause. Enter SMITH, *reflecting.*

SMITH   Was that pleasurable?
I certainly wanted it to be.
It is natural to want to seek pleasure in all the
    dreams one is forced to suppress
And he... he is certainly handsome
And masterful in a way that I enjoy.
But
Such coldness
Such coldness in his eyes
My new friends were not cold in the club.
They liked me. They really did.
We laughed and laughed
And I wasn't shy any more.
They thought it so funny when I said
I thought I was in paradise.
But he does not belong to paradise.
He comes from somewhere very cold.
I want to caress his cheek
I want to feel his face just brushing mine
But he just takes me to the privy
And has me bending over the seat.
He does it so fast
And then he says
'I aim to do fifteen today'

And then
'You're number twelve.'
And then he goes.
He never looked at me.

Pause.

The theory is.
The theory is our fellow feeling for each other,
Our sympathy,
That's what should govern our arrangement of
     society.
That the relationship between buyer and seller,
Being based on mutual advantage,
Will deepen and develop our common humanity.
The theory of moral sentiments.
I was proud of it.
Why was he so cold?
Perhaps Mother was right.
Perhaps all this is wickedness.
There's something wrong
There's something wrong
I never encountered anyone so cold.

He becomes aware of the audience.

Why aren't you happier
When you have so much?
What's wrong
And him so cold
So very cold.
Can I buy tenderness?

HUME   What is a reasonable man to do
              What is a reasonable man to say?
              Reason has nothing!
              Reason has nothing to say!

EVE   You're wrong, Mr Hume. I'm still reasoning.
              I haven't stopped reasoning!
              In a hospital bed, Mr Hume, with multiple
                   fractures,
              Immobilised.
              I had to think.

They said I could never have another child
But I did not care
I refused to care about that!
Why bring another child into this world!
Why did you do it, Mum?
Were you fit for it?
You made me think it was all my fault somehow.
But it wasn't. It wasn't me!
All you could think about was getting more
    money for the Scientologists
So you could rise up another grade.
She wanted to be clear, you see.
But she never got clear of him.
He came. Came to shout at me in my hospital bed.
He happened to be off the rigs just then.
He was drunk. They had to throw him off the
    ward.
You think you can trust your mum and dad but
There comes a time when you understand you can
    trust no one.
That you're on your own.
Early memories, Mr Hume
My early memories were my mum's head being
    bashed against a wall.
I must have thought it normal.
And that's why I put myself in the power of a man
    and almost died.
No more. No more of that!
And no more poverty. No more chaos!
I would not suffer that.
That's when I went to college, Mr Hume.
I got better and I bettered myself.
And I am proud of that. And then I left my home.
My mum was crying. It was cruel.
'Don't leave me,' she kept saying.
'Don't leave me here with him.
Don't leave me here alone.'
I went anyway.
And was I right?
Was I wrong?
I hardened my heart, Mr Hume.

Was I wrong to leave my family
Was I wrong to leave them all behind?

HUME   Madam, I was fortunate.
My family were loving and they were kind.
But I still had to leave them.
Leave them and find my path alone.

SMITH   Where's tenderness?
I'm looking on the machine
But I can't find it anywhere.
I can find tenderness in meat
Tenderness in the breasts
Signs and symptoms of a dread disease.
A film called tenderness.
A film. A film is a moving picture.
A picture that tells a story.
The story of a family and a brutal teenage killer.
Where is tenderness?
What kind of world is this?
What have we done?

EVE   Dog eat dog, Mr Smith.
That's how it was.
That's how it was.
That's how it always was, only I never saw it
Until I got up from my hospital bed
And started to make my own way in the world.

SMITH   Do you remember those creatures, Hume?
Those ragged wretches of our time?
The dark doorways where they plied their squalid
     trade?
In the dark doorways and stinking alleys of the
     Canongate?
As I made my daily walk from my home to the
     Customs House, every day up the Royal Mile,
I would have to walk past them.
I cultivated an abstracted air so I could avoid
     catching their eye.
And those with the spirit to laugh would mock me
     in my shyness.
They were desperate women, Hume, abandoned,

often in despair, whose misfortunes left them
no other option.
But now, Hume, now the market has expanded,
And so has the scope and range of their
operations.
People of every gender, Hume, people of none.
People of every age and class and nationality and
race.
As if the whole world, the whole world were
prostituting themselves!

EVE I was in the catering trade!
I made my money making banquets for bankers!
Helping them waste the money that they stole
from us.
That was before they dragged us all down to ruin.
And they did steal it, Mr Smith.
Stole it in your name.

SMITH I look for tenderness and I see a boy
Six years old.
His keeper boasts of it.
'Fresh flesh. Still untainted.
A good price. Innocent.'
The boy holds out his hands
Holds out his hands to me as he's been taught.
Holds out his hands.
And smiles.
In my name, Hume. In my name.
They call this niche marketing.
Where did we go wrong?
I have looked into it, Hume.
And I have seen.
I have seen what we have done.
The principal occupation of the world economy is
the trade in human flesh.
If not defiling it, then in destroying it.
Weaponry, Hume. Weaponry!
There's an endless market for that.
People in the know, Hume, recommend a GLOCK.
And they're so easy to obtain.
Ask this machine and it'll take you to a bar.

Not so very far from here in Edinburgh
Where you can buy one.
Buy it dry or buy it wet.
Wet is more expensive, Hume, because with the
        implement you also buy an operative.
And they'll do the job for you.
Buy it dry you have to do the job yourself.
Remember America, Hume, America
That hopeful experiment in equality
And liberty and the rights of man?
Now it's a place where you can buy machine guns
        off the shelf and go out and shoot as many as
        you like.
And competition makes the prices very keen.
The Invisible Hand.
The market's Invisible Hand that I imagined
Would guide us to enlightenment!
All I wanted, Hume, all I ever wanted was to think
        about the world!
I wanted it to be better!
Where did we go wrong?
I do not understand.

HUME   There there, Mr Smith. Don't cry.
            There is no need for tears.
            I'm sure reason will prevail.
            Reason and good sense and humanity.

SMITH   I burnt my books. Remember I asked you to.
            You refused.

HUME   How could I?
            How could I burn the products of so beautiful a
                mind?

SMITH   In one thing only was I correct.
            When I denounced the pernicious evil of currency
                speculation.
            The folly and destructiveness of banks!
            Drag out their leaders. Hang them from the bridges!
            Hang them all. And burn the banks!
            I burnt my books. Burnt them all. On 11th July.
            Hutton helped me.

In my garden. All of them.
All sixteen volumes. All except the two.
The two that I could not recall.
They should be rounded up and burnt!
Burn the market.
Burn it to the ground.
Start again. Start again with something else.
Use sympathy.
Burn the market.
Burn the books.
I did. On 11th July 1790.
In the garden of my house off the Canongate.
And that night I dined with my usual complacency.

SMITH *turns off his light.*

SMITH *has gone.*

HUME   It grieves me that you saw him thus.
What you saw did not do him justice.
He was the gentlest, kindest man,
With the most brilliant mind.
Would you join me in a dish of tea?
It is sometimes most consoling.
We are imperfect creatures, madam,
And it is only to be expected that we should use
        even our most perfect inventions for
        imperfect and unworthy ends.
This is the finest tea. From China.
Note how the market has united the farthest
        corners of the earth for mutual benefit and
        pleasure.
Madam, I drink to you.
I worked for a merchant once.
It was an early and my only attempt to live a
        normal life.
My employer, madam, was a certain Mr Michael
        Miller.
A merchant in Bristol. He was a brutish, forceful
        man. Wealthy. Very knowledgeable in his
        trade. I discovered that he dealt principally in
        slaves. But I did not object to that. What I
        could not abide was his disgraceful writing

style. Principally his lamentable misuse of the semicolon.

But when I courteously drew this to his attention, he informed me in the coarsest terms that his writing style made him twenty thousand a year and that he saw no reason to change it.

Then he dismissed me.

And I am sure he was right. I was only his junior clerk.

And had I stayed I would have accomplished nothing of value at all.

I would simply have made money.

It is strange, madam, how often what appears to us to be the greatest misfortune can in the end work out to our greatest good.

More tea?

Dear madam, dear Miss Eve, would you so greatly object were I to hold your hand?

Rest assured, I seek no sexual gratification of any kind. It is simply that human contact can be so very comforting.

There.

The world, Miss Eve, is vast, lonely,

And often comfortless.

There is such solace in a human touch.

And now, if you'll permit me, may we indulge a certain curiosity that I have to gaze into Mr Smith's machine?

Thank you.

I see...

I see a man with white hair and a bushy moustache.

He tells me his name is Einstein. Very well.

He says:

'Time is space.

Space is time.'

I understand. I understand!

'I followed you in breaking things down.

Breaking things down into their component parts.

And we can do this.

Breaking the world down,

Breaking the world down into smaller and smaller
    pieces.
Into the cell, the molecule.
Into the atom.
It is not solid.
Inside the atom is so much empty space.
Inside each atom is another universe.
And there, at the very base of everything,
Lies incalculable power.'
And he looks at me.
I see his huge sad eyes.
And then:
'I see Shiva. The destroyer of worlds.'
And then he's gone.
Desolation. Ruin.
A name: Hi Ro Shi Ma.
Then emptiness.
A fat man laughing underneath a tree.
Holding a lotus flower.
'The world is the creation of the mind'
He says, and he's holding out the flower.
'There is an end,' he says,
'An end to human suffering.
Compassion is the key.'
I take the flower.
He greets me like a brother,
And
I
Am
Gone.

EVE *is alone.*

EVE   I see the world.
I see it hanging in the universe.
Tenderly.
So beautiful.
So vulnerable.
So alone.
Oh wonder.
As I get closer it gets huger
Huger and huger

But I can tell
It is made up of the smallest things.
Oh look, there's me.
I'm just a child.
It's my first day of nursery, and I've been given a
    clean white smock. With blue flowers on it.
And a peg of my own to hang it on.
And a beautiful clean facecloth to wash my face
    with.
I come from a place where there's shouting and
    banging and fighting and nothing is ever safe
    or right.
So this place feels like Heaven.
On Sundays,
There's a priest tells me about Heaven.
He's tall and black and tells me about the Garden
    of Eden and the apple of the Tree of
    Knowledge and how bad it was of Eve to pick
    it.
I have to say yes, yes she was very bad,
But secretly, in my deepest heart, I feel very
    proud.
Because somehow I think I did it.
Seeking knowledge is not a crime.
People need to know.
When we moved into our Glenrothes house it was
    enormous.
We used to have just the one room, and now there
    were five. We had no furniture to put in them.
The empty dirty rooms made me ashamed and I
    could never invite my friends in.
And the windows were bare.
Ours was the only house in the street which had
    empty windows.
And people pointed fingers and made cruel
    remarks.
But if they'd known what we went through.
If they'd eaten the apple and if they'd known
Then they would never have been so unkind.

Slowly we have begun to see the world.

The world hanging in deep space.

We hear the music of the spheres.

These were two men who ate the fruit and I have
        eaten it too.
We all have.
They needed to see us
And we needed to see them.
And now they've gone.
Life is so very short.
Ladies and gentlemen, forgive our faults.
Forgive your own.
Farewell.

End.

A Nick Hern Book

The Tree of Knowledge first published in Great Britain as a paperback original in 2011 by Nick Hern Books Limited, 14 Larden Road, London W3 7ST, in association with the Traverse Theatre, Edinburgh

The Tree of Knowledge copyright © 2011 Jo Clifford

Jo Clifford has asserted her right to be identified as the author of this work

Cover photograph by Laurence Winram
Cover design by Ned Hoste, 2H

Typeset by Nick Hern Books, London
Printed in Great Britain by Mimeo Ltd, Huntingdon, Cambridgeshire PE29 6XX

A CIP catalogue record for this book is available from the British Library

ISBN 978 1 84842 235 3